15 HINTS TO
ENTREPRENEURIAL SUCCESS
Lessons From A Caribbean Business Woman

Heneka Watkis-Porter

AuthorHouse™ LLC
1663 Liberty Drive
Bloomington, IN 47403
www.authorhouse.com
Phone: 1-800-839-8640

Published by AuthorHouse   04/10/2014

ISBN: 978-1-4918-7384-7 (sc)
ISBN: 978-1-4918-7385-4 (hc)
ISBN: 978-1-4918-7386-1 (e)

Library of Congress Control Number: 2014905213

CONTENTS

Acknowledgements vii

Foreword...ix

Preface...xi

Introduction xiii

Finding Your Purpose... 3

Defining Success... 15

Evicting Fear 21

Preparation, Preparation, Preparation 25

Perspective... 29

Perseverance... 33

Getting (and staying) Motivated 37

Being A River Not A Reservoir... 39

Reliability... 41

Customer Service.. 45

Marketing 47

Financials... 53

Intellectual Property 55

Negotiation 57

Planning... 61

Appendix 63

ACKNOWLEDGEMENTS

I wish to express my deepest gratitude to the following:

To God for His constant guidance every step of the way while providing me with the strength to keep going, inspiring me to continue to the end.

To the staff at Author House Publishing for being so professional from the very first call to completion of this book; you made publishing so seamless.

To Adolph Porter for being a wonderful husband, your continued love and support keep me going; your sense of humour is priceless.

To Pastor and friend Reverend L. Christopher Mason for your constant words of encouragement; they have helped to strengthen me.

To the Portmore United Church's intercessors for your many prayers; to Reverend Lavene Elliot and the team at Unleashing Purpose Ministries, much love and thanks for the continuous support.

To Pastor, friend and mentor Reverend Joel Downer, you have inspired me to be the best I can be. You have helped a great deal in building self-confidence.

To Business Services Organizations (BSOs) that have nurtured my development over the years especially to JAMPRO, JIPO, JBDC,

CEDA and to mentors Action Coach's Marcia Woon-Choy and National Baking Company's Steven Sykes and the rest of the team, thanks for your invaluable support.

To Owen James for your wisdom, guidance and belief in me; I owe you a debt of gratitude.

To Corine LaFont for encouraging me to "just start writing" and for narrowing down a subject area when there were so many ideas floating around in my head.

To friends and supporters too numerous to mention by name; you believed in me, but especially Nicole Lynch I couldn't have done it without your cheers. I owe you a debt of gratitude.

To my fellow *"I Believe Initiative"* (IBI) Ambassador Glenford Smith for your guidance and insight along the way.

To the "IBI" team who have provided another platform for me to share my story and to provide encouragement to others as I live my purpose of "Life Transformation through Inspiration," thank you.

His Excellency the Most Honourable Sir Patrick Allen, our Governor-General, who brought the IBI into being and continues to inspire youth with its positive messages and programmes, has greatly honoured me by writing the foreword for my book. A million thanks, Your Excellency!

FOREWORD

In 2012, Heneka Watkis-Porter began her journey with the "I Believe" Initiative IBI), first as a Youth Conference Presenter and later as one of the founding "I Believe" Ambassadors. The same drive to motivate others to excellence which prompted her participation in the IBI has propelled her into writing this book. In it, she poignantly shares memories of a life in which she was abused even in the womb, but which, with God's help, have become her launching pad to higher achievements. Heneka is the epitome of the IBI message: she has seized the good in her life to right the wrong.

This book was written with young businesspersons—or those wanting to venture in business—in mind. Heneka begins where it matter most: a sense of purpose and a determination to press on to the finish line, despite the hurdles on the way. One of my favourite lines in her book is *"A life of purpose enables us to awake each day ready to seize every opportunity that presents itself and to create opportunities where none seem to exist."* She is not writing theory: this is her life experience!

Heneka's objective is to prove to young and aspiring businesspersons that like her, who began life with so many disadvantages, they can dream big and realize their goals. Success will come by a dint of preparation, purpose, perseverance and a passion for focused, effective work. She shares tips which have helped her in her quest for success. Importantly, this includes information on financial planning and management, a weakness of several micro and small businesses, as well as on negotiation and marketing, among others which are sure to be helpful to the potential entrepreneur.

I am very pleased to endorse this first book by "I Believe" Ambassador Heneka Watkis-Porter who shares my passion that *there is nothing wrong with Jamaica that cannot be fixed by what is right with Jamaica".*

His Excellency the Most Honourable Sir Patrick L. Allen, ON, GCMG, CD
Governor-General of Jamaica
King's House
Kingston
March, 2014

PREFACE

It is recorded that 377,000 babies were born on Wednesday, June 7, 1978.

Among this number, was a baby girl born to a bewildered and confused 16-year old. Prior to this birth, the girl's mother would often utter these words to her desperate and traumatized teenager, "a wish wen di pickney a bawn it tun crass way an kill yuh."

With no support from the man who was equally responsible for her being in that state and with very little family support, it must have taken all the inner strength this teen could muster not to have an abortion; only to get to the delivery room weeks after to be asked by a nurse: "What's all the fuss about? It's just a baby!"

A baby that would later grow to hear words such as "yuh nah kum out to nutt'n good; anyting too black nuh good." A baby that would later grow to become close friends with feelings of rejection, despondency, hurt and pain. A child that would be made to feel that she was ugly. A child that would meet her father when she was 11 years old; a little girl who never felt the love of parents; a girl that would later grow with little or no self worth or confidence. That baby would grow to attempt suicide and to experience abuse of all sorts.

That baby was me.

Faced with all odds against me, I made the conscious decision to make lemonade with my lemons. I refused to let my past be a hindrance to my future. I decided to live each day with expectancy, working towards becoming the best me possible.

INTRODUCTION

My entrepreneurial journey began in 2007. It didn't take long for me to recognize that my success or not would be dependent on my mind-set and perspective on life in general. It became clear to me that in order to get ahead I would have to be resolute in my mind that there is no limit; not even the sky. If I saw the sky as a limit, then my natural lazy mind would kick in and believe that once I reached a certain level, then I would have reached my summit. I wasn't going to do that to myself. I knew there was no limit and that kept me going on and on and on.

I have come to terms with the fact that as a young person I am not the future of this world; I am part of the now, the present; the one to make a difference. I am, in fact, the change that I seek.

A positive approach to life despite not having the colour of connection, a rich spouse or influential friends made a world of difference in building the **Patwa** brand and later **10 Fyah Side**. It wasn't always easy to think positive though. Negative thoughts seemed to appear without any effort. I had to train my mind to replace negative thoughts with ones that are aligned to success.

When I made the decision to quit working for other people a few years ago, writing was primary amongst the list of reasons. I wanted to share my experiences with others. If I can help at least one person as I live my life's purpose of *"transformation through inspiration,"* then part of my mission would have been accomplished.

The message I want to drive home by the time you reach the end of this book, is that we all have God-given talents and abilities; all are placed on this earth for a reason. So then, let us take the steps that are necessary on a daily basis to be one step closer to our dreams.

In the same way I know that greatness lies within me and that I am unstoppable, I know it is true for everyone who believes. This is why I am more than proud to be part of the Governor General's *I Believe Initiative* (IBI). At his inauguration as Governor-General in February 2009, His Excellency the Most Honourable Sir Patrick Allen declared: "there is nothing wrong with Jamaica that cannot be fixed by what is right with Jamaica", giving birth to the IBI. This message is in no way limited to this beautiful land of wood and water, but certainly extends to the entire globe.

There is so much positivity, potential and purpose in all of us; if only we would induce labour and give birth to them. I believe, therefore I promise. Do you?

Along my entrepreneurial journey I have identified several keys to my success over a relatively short space of time. Talking with other successful people has revealed that these attributes are in no way limited to me. Whosoever will may come and be part of the movement. I will share fifteen (15) of these along with some personal anecdotes to illustrate these pointers.

'Section One' explores:

1. Finding Your Purpose
2. Defining Success
3. Evicting Fear
4. Preparation, Preparation, Preparation
5. Perspective
6. Perseverance
7. Getting & Staying Motivated
8. Being a River not a Reservoir
9. Reliability

'Section Two' examines more conventional business subject matters as follow:

1. Customer Service
2. Marketing
3. Financials
4. Intellectual Property
5. Negotiation
6. Planning

Being an entrepreneur has as much to do with attitude as it does supply and demand. In order to be successful at this challenging yet rewarding endeavour, we must make every effort to work at becoming our best selves. While this may sound easy to do, it does take continuous effort. We have to work constantly at being better men and women of this wonderful world.

The things we do are merely the tip of the iceberg. They are driven by what we cannot see. Our desire for love, security, significance, growth and connection are the main drivers. Different individuals are driven by different needs or a different set of needs in varying degrees. What we believe is impacted by the values and morals we embrace. Our interpretation of what is happening at the moment creates a platform for these values. You see, we can only achieve what we believe and what we believe has much to do with our experiences and encounters, events, education and our environments. These factors play significant roles in defining our thought processes and by extension, our accomplishments in our field of choice. Let's examine some of these internal aspects and their connection to our growth.

SECTION 1

FINDING YOUR PURPOSE

There exist copious amounts of written materials on the subject matter of *purpose*. The dynamic and charismatic Bishop T.D. Jakes often says, "Everything happens when you find your purpose and nothing happens before you do."

Still, for Author and Motivational Speaker Myles Munroe, "The greatest tragedy in life is not death, but life without a purpose." It may seem strange to discuss the topic of purpose in a book about entrepreneurial success. However, you shouldn't read for long before you find it's not so farfetched after all.

What is this thing called purpose anyway? What is this overarching fascination with what seems to be a buzz word for every motivational speaker, life coach and transformational leader?

Simply put, it is that gut feeling, inclination or calling to a life's vocation that fuels passion and drive in an individual. It is that one thing that we were created to do and to live by; it is that burning desire to do the thing that gives us satisfaction. If we do otherwise, invariably we are faced with emotional instability, discomfort and heartache.

That we have been given the gift of life for a reason is an argument held to be true by many. Probably nine out of every ten persons have at one point or another asked the question, "Why am I here?" For some, the answer unfolded mere years after exiting the womb;

some when they got to middle age; yet others when they were quite close to the tomb. Sadly there are those who died without ever knowing; without ever exposing the world to their leadership, skills and talent, to that one special thing that only they alone were created to execute.

Each of us has been given talents and skills that are unique to us. Sometimes we are unable to be purposeful because we are caught up with trying to be all things to all people. We are busy trying to develop our weaknesses instead of focusing on our strengths. This is one sure way to miss the mark of why we are here.

What is the practical manifestation of a life without purpose? People who aren't living on purpose are often unexcited about waking up in the mornings. They get anxious about facing the day ahead, probably to get to a job executing functions that deplete their energy. Life for them begins to feel like a rat race, merely existing and not living. There can be no joy in that kind of life. Steve Jobs knew how to deal with this existence. He said, "For the past 33 years, I have looked in the mirror every morning and asked myself: 'If today were the last day of my life, would I want to do what I am about to do today?' And whenever the answer has been 'No' for too many days in a row, I know I need to change something."

I have asked myself this question on numerous occasions. In December, 2010; I became frustrated and uncomfortable with the status quo of going to a job I no longer felt fulfilled doing. After much praying and deliberation, I acted on the most profound response I could ever ask for. Reading my daily subscription of the devotional, *The Daily Hope*—from the author of *Purpose Driven*

Life, Rick Warren, I got yet another response to my many months of questioning my next move. This particular morning's edition was written by Tom Holladay, a pastor at Warren's Saddleback Church in Southern California. The title of the devotional had me in awe. It stated, *"Obeying God Requires You Take a Risk."* If for one moment I thought the title of the devotional was just a mere coincidence, toward the end of it, *". . . that risk of faith could mean . . . leaving your job"* sealed the deal for me. I eventually decided to walk away from the security of full-time employment a few months after in February, 2011.

It took all the strength I had to do this; to walk away from the security of paid vacation, sick leave, health insurance, pension plan, subsidized lunch and the whole shebang. It wasn't easy, but it had to be done!

It is important to remember that emotions and moods are fickle. While we may not always feel as though on top of the world even when we are doing what we are called to do, undoubtedly we live each moment embracing the joys of life with a sense of gratitude for each day that passes and the experiences that accompany them. A life of purpose enables us to awake each day ready to seize every opportunity that presents itself and to create opportunities where none seem to exist. Every day for us becomes a wonderful day to be breathing.

As you go through your days, a good habit to develop is to check your mood temperature to determine how purposeful your life is. Do you experience them in extreme? If you cannot answer with a resounding 'no' then chances are you are not living on purpose.

While a life of purpose will not always guarantee you a life free from lows, when they surface, you will be able to snap out of them quickly. Instead of throwing pity parties, you take moments to be grateful for the small things in life such as the chirping of birds, the flowering of a plant, and the swaying of a tree limb or a simple business idea being brought to life.

When you're living on purpose, you're fulfilled because you're living a life engulfed in personal meaning. You stop questioning your reason for existence and instead embrace every moment of your life and the path you have chosen. Life becomes beautiful.

Only a life lived on purpose is a fulfilled life. A life of purpose prevents you from being an enemy to yourself; you will know better than to underestimate the power of words. You will believe in the power of positive thinking and self-fulfilling prophecy and choose to speak positively about yourself at all times, because whatever you believe about yourself is truth.

How many of us while growing up have heard words like, "you'll never amount to anything?" In Jamaica, family members sometimes tell the children in their families that "you're just like yuh wutliss puppa." Those are words that pierce deeper that any sword could and can either make or break you depending on your mind-set. It takes practice to replace those negative words reverberating in your psyche with positive ones.

To erase one negative word spoken, it takes repeating a positive word many more times. It is important to think and speak positively at all times as you strive to fulfill your destiny. At all costs, avoid speaking negatively about yourself and those around you. Forget the painful negative words you may have heard at the varying stages of your life. You have the power to control your thoughts; take them captive and believe only the positive ones. Sift the negative ones out and cast them aside.

The power of words is undeniably strong; the tongue is a powerful sword. It is imperative to speak positively into your life even when others are saying otherwise; write affirmations and repeat them daily stating them in the NOW.

For example if your goal is to be the owner of a multi-billion dollar business, say "I AM the owner of a multi-billion dollar corporation." In the beginning it might sound crazy but as you keep saying it, you get used to it and start believing. Because you BELIEVE, you DO the necessary actions to make it a reality. You will be amazed how things begin to unfold right before your eyes. Many of the things that are happening in my life now are things that I believed and affirmed would manifest such as starting a business, writing a book, creating a hosting my radio shows and travelling the world among other things.

Peace and purpose are inextricably linked. Only a mind that is at ease with its calling can categorically claim to be at peace. Focusing on things with intrinsic value will help to provide that calming sense of serenity.

Money does not bring happiness. Resist the temptation to focus your life solely on making a dollar. It does not push you beyond your limit nor does it challenge you. Living for something greater than money provides personal gratification in a way that is sometimes hard to explain. The ability to put a smile on another person's face gives a deeper meaning to life for example. This is what makes the world a better place amidst all the hurt and pain facing the human race.

If you are not already living on purpose, your desire to get there will lead you to a point where you begin to feel uncomfortable. There will come a point when the status quo is no longer acceptable. It is alright to get comfortable feeling uncomfortable; think of the caterpillar during its period of metamorphosis—from egg to larva to pupa and then into an adult—a beautiful butterfly. Gold goes through the fire to be refined.

When you combine your strengths with your passions there is no limit to where your life will go. Identify what it is that you can do even with your eyes closed. What moments are you happiest? Embark on a hero's journey and do that which you were made for. To borrow the words of gospel recording artiste Alvin Slaughter, "Launch out into the deep, let your faith take you somewhere you've never been before." Whatever it is, just do it!

Living a life of purpose prevents you from falling into the trap of craving the validation of others. When you know who you are and what your reason for life is, it doesn't matter if others don't believe in you. Your self confidence gets bigger than any one person's belief in you.

We must never rely on people's opinion which could prevent us from soaring to the height of our vocations. Know too, that in life there will be those who will journey with you only to a point of their own anticipation of where you will end up. The moment you surpass where they originally thought you would have reached, they may no longer celebrate with you. They have put limitations on themselves and by extension have also placed the same on you. Don't succumb to this trap. Run!

While there is no standard blueprint to follow in identifying one's purpose, there are some factors which remain constant in the pursuit of purpose. Here are some sure signs that you are living a life that was meant specifically for you:

O It is true that if you love what you do, you will never have to work a day in your life. When you truly love what you are doing you will be excited about doing it. The result is an obsession that is almost inexplicable and you enjoy every moment of it. This gives you joy and a true sense of reason for living. In the moments you feel like you want to stay in bed and simply let time pass by, there is a constant reminder of the reasons not to and your energy comes from that. It doesn't matter how exhausted I am, I always have more energy to pursue aspects of my entrepreneurial quest without it ever feeling like work.

O There are times others may be trying to get your attention but you are so focused it appears that there is no one around. You are always focused when doing what you love. You do not allow yourself to get distracted. 'Random' social events will not appeal to you much, as your gaze is affixed on your prize.

O You have a strong underlying belief that you are doing what you were created for. You may have tried several things before and soon found that your interest in them disappeared as quickly as they came.

○ You keep a clear vision all the time of where you want to reach irrespective of any 'failure' that may happen along the way.

○ Even with a clear vision, there are times you are not quite sure of what to do. As chapters unfold and phases roll out and define themselves, you stay open to guidance from professionals, books, CDs, the internet or whatever resource is available to you. Although it is your purpose, you will never be able to accomplish it alone. Forging strategic alliances with the right people and organizations and having the right tools, is a sure way to get ahead. I have aligned myself to many business services and other organizations. For example, my association with JAMPRO has enabled me to be exposed to capacity building, access to markets and many other valuable resources and have established me as a bona-fide entrepreneur. Caribbean Export Development Agency (CEDA) is another strategic alliance I have formed, obtaining grants, training and market penetration opportunities. I also rely much on inspiration from online resources.

○ You keep going when the going gets tough; in those times when things don't seem to be going right. The odds all appear to be stacked up against you; yet you refuse to give up because you know that anything that is worth fighting for usually comes with challenges. I recall when my business was located in a space that was not ideal for my type of business. It felt as though everything and everyone was working against me. Yet I refused to give up. I later found an ideal location after months of what felt like punishment. In retrospect, being uncomfortable in that former location was the best thing that could have happened to me as it provided the opportunity to find somewhere more suitable.

O You surprise even yourself at your persistence and drive to press on. Challenges are inevitable; it is how you deal with them that will determine whether you are doing what you were called to do. Despite the challenges, hurdles, trials, tribulations and frustrations, you look in retrospect with delight knowing that you have totally enjoyed the experience anyway and have no regrets. The mistakes were merely to teach you lessons. You say to yourself, these mistakes only meant that you tried something new. I have learnt that challenges are just educational tools to teach you how to circumnavigate and manipulate your situations as you move forward. Without them, you would never develop the backbone and stamina required to become successful in your endeavours.

O Sometimes you find that many of the opportunities that are aligned to your purpose just seem to fall into place easily and things appear to 'just happen'. The telephone calls, emails, connections and people just seem to appear serendipitously to give guidance and assistance; things that seem to happen out of the apparent blue. The truth is, nothing happens by chance. I could provide so many examples of persons just reaching out to me, providing guidance and assistance in any way they can, because they recognize the passion with which I am in pursuit of my goal.

When I went on a Study Tour to Manchester, Berlin and Paris in 2012, it was partly because on separate occasions, representatives from JAMPRO inquired whether or not I had submitted an application to CEDA to be part of this opportunity. I had decided I wouldn't submit an application because I didn't think I met all the criteria. A few weeks after making their deadline based on the recommendation from JAMPRO, I received a letter which read:

"RE: *Official Invitation to participate in a Study Tour in Europe for Caribbean business people from the Cultural Industries.*

"Thank you for your expression of interest in the Study Tour of Cultural Industries for Caribbean business people that Caribbean Export Development Agency (CEDA) is facilitating. The ACP Business Climate facility (BizClim) and CEDA are pleased to sponsor your attendance at this event."

Clearly, the weight placed on the areas in which I qualified was enough to render me successful. I was more than thankful that I had taken the advice of those ladies.

O Another important sign is that you realize what you do make a real difference in the lives of others around you. Part of the reason it is important to find your purpose is that "no man is an island, no man stands alone." The real value of what you do is manifested when others are able to say "thank you." For example, it was no doubt my involvement in business that gave me the platform to become an IBI Ambassador. The fact that I have the opportunity to influence others and experience the gratitude of the recipients is enough to keep me motivated.

DEFINING SUCCESS

A person's definition of success is in large part dependent on his mores and values. It is important to arrive at your own definition of success; have a definiteness of purpose; know what is important to you. Be clear what you want to accomplish and carefully strategize how to accomplish it. How will family, finance, business, wellness, spirituality, marriage, extra-curricular activities, social life and hobbies score in your definition? Having definite goals in mind will help determine where you are on your chart of success.

Part of this journey includes assessing your current position with respect to all the variables that are important to you and then setting goals outlining where you want to be within a stated time frame.

The goals that you set must be SMART; i.e. **S**pecific, **M**easurable, **A**ttainable, **R**ealistic and **T**imely. To get a specific goal some 'w' questions will have to be answered, namely: who, why, what, when, which and where are critical. Dig deep to ascertain these.

Next, establish concrete criteria for measuring progress. When you measure, you stay on track, reach your target dates and experience a sense of fulfillment with each milestone achieved. In determining whether your goal is measurable you must ask questions such as "How much? How many? How will I know when it is accomplished?"

When you identify goals that are meaningful to you, you begin to look for ways to make them come through. You will develop the ability to see previously overlooked opportunities. When you carefully plan your next move, goals that once appeared unattainable, seem closer within your grasp.

To be realistic, a goal must be an objective to which you are both 'willing and able' to work towards. A goal can be both high and realistic at the same time. Usually when we have a low goal, there is also a low motivation. Many persons can testify to the fact that some of their most difficult tasks were the ones in which they were most successful, simply because they were labors of love.

Finally, a goal should be set within a specific time frame and is tangible, with the ability to be experienced with one of the 5 senses. When do you need to accomplish this by? If I need to lose weight, I need to indicate how much and by when. My subconscious will then kick in to start doing the things to make this a reality.

Success is relative and is really what you define it to be. According to Bradley Sugars, CEO of the world's number one business coaching firm, Action Coach, "A business is a commercially profitable enterprise that can run without me." Success must be seen as more than just the tangibles such as money in the bank, a nice car and house. If you are a business owner, you are most successful when you are able to manage your time and have the accompanying resources necessary to help to improve the life of others. The ability to spend time with family and friends, take vacations, etc without compromising the growth of your business, is a sign that you are on your way to becoming successful.

The fact that I get to do other things that are not necessarily business related weighs heavily on my definition of success. Opportunities to volunteer, write, develop and create programs among others, keep me excited and motivated. I see these as part of my success.

In your quest to accomplish your goals, ensure that your success does not come at the expense of others. We should go after our goals by any means necessary without infringing on our values and the laws of the land. Ill-gotten gain is never worth the price paid to get it. We must be able to live with our consciences and others peaceably in the midst of our success. Then and only then are we truly successful.

Successful people are not easily distracted by negativity. As you become more successful, you will begin to master the art of ignoring distractions and so focus intensely on your life's definite major purpose.

Don't think about the limits and barriers to success which exist only in the mind to the extent that you allow it to. Successful people learn to master the art of auto suggestion—calling those things that are not as though they are. Whatever we speak becomes embedded in our subconscious. Concentrate on succeeding, not on the possibility of failure.

Start believing that you have a right to success and you will do the things that are necessary to get you there.

It is important to understand why we do the things we do. Everyone's path to success is different regardless of the area of choice that we decide to embark on. If entrepreneurship is your thing, there could be any number of reasons that propelled you there. One thing should be clear; you must identify your 'why' for doing what you have decided to do. This fundamental reason will keep you grounded when your ship appears to be sinking. The moments of turbulence will be but a mere shadow in the grand scheme of things.

Let your why be your starting point; this will be a major driving force for everything else.

Your why is simply that, your underlying reason for your decisions about what you embark upon. Make it known from the get go. My "why" is simply a strong desire to make a difference in the life of my family; to shift away from the circumstances that I encountered whilst growing up. I see it as my personal responsibility to break this vicious generational cycle of lack. Of course, I am in business to make a profit but no less is my aspiration to make a difference in the lives of those who believe there is no hope. I must inspire and motivate them.

It may sound a bit simplistic but when you think about it, many persons get up from day to day just doing things out of second nature without ever questioning their reasons for doing them.

Your why could simply be your desire to make this world a better place through social responsibility. Using your business as a vehicle for this can be rewarding.

Knowing your why comes from a place of passion. Robert Kyosaki *et al*, author of *Rich Dad Poor Dad* defines passion as "A combination of love and hate." He explained that you have to hate something strong enough to want to avoid it which will in turn drive you to accomplish the thing you love.

Part of the importance of knowing your why lies in the fact that life is a journey and with it comes challenges which may seem insurmountable at times. When these challenges arise, you will need to remember why you made your choice to begin with. This underlying reason will help to motivate you to get ahead, instead of quitting for an easier way out.

Your why is one of the most important parts of your journey; it will help you become an over-comer in order to succeed in your life's choices.

EVICTING FEAR

One of the greatest, if not the greatest hindrance to persons stepping out of their comfort zone and entering the unknown is FEAR (False Expectations Appearing Real). It is human nature to fear what we do not know. Make a conscious decision to fear nothing. The only thing you should fear is fear itself, run from it!

I speak from a position of experience. Once I began contemplating business full-time, it took me several months to make the life-changing decision. The decision to quit full time employment whilst working at an organization in the shipping industry was not an easy one.

I was fearful of the uncertainty that comes with running a business full time. No longer would there be the security of a guaranteed monthly salary, sick days, paid vacation, health insurance and all the other benefits associated with employment. I was scared to death of doing it. I didn't let fear cripple me though; I was fierce, ferocious and fearless. Though it wasn't easy, I eventually replaced my fear with faith, and began to live not by what is evident before me, but by my hope of a successful future.

A fitting, powerful and profound excerpt comes from United States Author and Lecturer, Marianne Williamson:

'Our deepest fear is not that we are inadequate. Our deepest fear is that we are powerful beyond measure. It

21

is our light, not our darkness that most frightens us. We ask ourselves, who am I to be brilliant, gorgeous, talented, and fabulous? Actually, who are you *not* to be? You are a child of God. Your playing small does not serve the world. There is nothing enlightened about shrinking so that other people will not feel insecure around you. We are all meant to shine, as children do. We were born to make manifest the glory of God that is within us. It is not just in some of us; it is in everyone and as we let our own light shine, we unconsciously give others permission to do the same. As we are liberated from our own fear, our presence automatically liberates others'.

Truth is, less than 10% of the things we fear in life actually do happen. Don't ignore your dreams because you are afraid to move on. In moving ahead, it is critical to be a visionary in order to become a winner. Going against the grain and being an outside of the box thinker is one way to set yourself apart from everybody else as you walk in your life's purpose and destiny. Procrastination is the theft of time. Stop procrastinating and start living your purpose; you owe it to yourself and your family.

Every profitable venture starts with an idea. It is your lack of fear and your confidence that will determine whether you move forward from one point to the next.

To win big you must be willing to fail big. Failure can be just a bump on the road to victory.

The world is not short of people with ideas; the issue usually is about moving from the point of hallucination to execution.

The idea that opposite attracts does not hold true when it comes to our thoughts. Quite on the contrary, "like attracts like"; "birds of a feather flock together"; "show me your company and I show you who you are." In the execution of your ideas, it is important to connect with like minds to bounce ideas off. Remember, people who are negative do not believe in their own abilities let alone have the guts to believe in yours.

They sabotage themselves with negative words. They think the worst is going to happen to them at all times. They are crippled by fear. They believe the world is out to get them. Full of self-pity and self-hate, they see themselves as victims and never victors. They blame themselves and others for everything that has ever gone wrong. They hang on to every single hurt and pain that has ever come their way. They can never move forward; and the cycle goes on.

I am emphasizing the importance of speaking positively over the things concerning your life. Our past defines our future only to the extent that we allow it. The mistakes we've made shouldn't be a hindrance to our growth. All persons with a desire to learn make mistakes; it is a natural part of growth. Where we are from and who our parents are, should have no business interfering with our present and our future. We should never allow the fear of taking calculated risks to stagnate us.

Entrepreneurship in particular is a huge risk but the rewards are greater than anything you could ever possibly lose. It is the fear of losing that keeps many people from diving into the deep end. Champions know adversity is the catalyst of mental toughness. You will never know the person you can be if pressure, tension and discipline are taken out of your life. T.S. Elliott puts it succinctly, "Only those who will risk going too far, can possibly find out how far they can go."

Develop the discipline of challenging yourself; see how far you can go. Great ones will always choose discipline over pleasure. Henry Ward Beecher says "Hold yourself responsible for a higher standard than anybody else expects of you."

Never excuse yourself. Never pity yourself. Be a hard master to yourself and be lenient to everybody else. Having the right mindset then is critical to being successful.

If your primary school was anything like mine, this quote from Henry Wadsworth Longfellow was implanted in your system and for a good reason too—"The heights by great men reached and kept were not attained by sudden flight; but they, while their companions slept were toiling upwards through the night." This is a great reminder that success is not an overnight phenomenon but something that is constantly worked at. We have to prepare!

PREPARATION, PREPARATION, PREPARATION

An integral factor in our development is our mental preparation. We must constantly train our minds to expect successful outcomes. It is true that as a man thinks, so is he. We become only what we think over time. Whether we believe we can or can't, we are correct.

Have you noticed how some people remain in the very same place year in, year out? They are always complaining that things are bad and that the economy is in a poor state. They never seem to have anything positive to say.

When we think, we release vibrations into the atmosphere to attract to us the very things that we think about. We must learn to get into the habit of thinking about the things we want to accomplish and writing down these goals and dreams. In order to be successful, it doesn't stop here; we must go further by taking these plans and reviewing them regularly then DOING what is necessary to make them a reality.

I like the strategy of Abraham Lincoln. He said if you gave him six (6) hours to cut down a tree, he would spend the first four (4) hours sharpening his axe. Intrinsic in his argument is that preparation is a main key to success. No doubt we have heard it said time and again that if you fail to prepare then be prepared to fail. It is not just a nicely sounding cliché, it is a fact.

Know that the fulfillment of any dream requires a relentless pursuit of one's goal and objectives. You have to become so obsessed with whatever it is you want to accomplish that it consumes your every waking moment. When you feel like giving up, it is at that moment you need to hold on with an even firmer grip. The joy and satisfaction come from knowing you have succeeded despite all odds being stacked up against you.

The celebrated Usain Bolt has the admiration of the world and he is deserving of it. In 2002, a stadium full of track and field enthusiasts watched as he effortlessly completed his 100M race at the World Junior Championships.

Bolt's relentless pursuit of gold; his heart evidently set on winning the race left the entire stadium in awe and admiration. It was there that many Jamaicans fell in love with him; not just because of his well-built physique, but his relentless pursuit of victory. Shortly after, sports analysts were not so kind to him when he began to suffer injuries and could not deliver as he had done before. Still, Bolt knew what he wanted to accomplish; he worked hard; he prepared; he persevered. Now the world knows who this wonder of an athlete Mr. Bolt is. He never saw himself as a victim, he saw instead a victor.

When we think about other athletes who pursue sports, we know that without diligent training they would be foolhardy to expect great results. How could they, if they failed to train, ate the foods they should not, and are downright undisciplined?

It is no different when it comes on to other disciplines within our pursuit. There are similar traits running as common threads among successful people. Commitment and dedication are important. There are days when you may not be able to see your way through; days when there are no blue skies visible and all there seem to be is the midnight hour. These days should serve as motivators knowing that the darkest hour is just before dawn.

The valley is not a place that we enjoy visiting. We become anxious and filled with concerns when things are not going our way; when we just can't seem to get ahead. Just know though, that if you persevere, your day of rejoicing will follow your moments of trials and tribulations. In order to truly appreciate the mountain top experience, there has to be some familiarity with the valley.

Take the example of another inspiring product of the Jamaican soil; vocal powerhouse Tessanne Chin. Acting on the advice of international recording artiste Orville 'Shaggy' Burrell, who has the ability to spot a diamond in the rough, Chin decided in 2013 to enter season 5 of the American pop competition, *The Voice*. After many rounds she emerged victorious, but her victory was not overnight. Singing was, in her words, her "bread and butter" for many years within the Jamaican music industry without getting the acknowledgement she deserved. Imagine if she had given up when her career seemed much like being on a tread mill? She was being prepared for her moment of victory.

After listening to her interviews, it became clear that she takes what she does very seriously. She sings her heart out regardless of the size of her audience. With all the advice in the world, Chin would not have won *The Voice* if she wasn't prepared. Opportunity doesn't come until we are ready for it. Clearly on **The Voice**, "opportunity met preparation" for Chin.

Undoubtedly, a relentless pursuit of success means that there is an opportunity cost to pay. The immediate gratification which comes from hanging out with friends or partying will have to be traded for a more permanent, long-term benefit.

As an entrepreneur for example, you spend time in the early years doing what others won't do so that in later years you get to do what others can't afford to. The sacrifice I'd say is definitely is worth it.

PERSPECTIVE

How do you look at life in general? What's your perspective? Is your glass half full or half empty? How do you view things and situations that are presented before your eyes?

If someone doesn't treat you the way you expect, do you say they are against you or is it that they are for themselves? Do you climb a mountain so that the world can see you, or so that you can see the world?

Instead of saying "I'm broke," saying "my cash flow needs improving" is a more positive alternative of indicating your status.

Life is really what you make it to be. Imagine two young men walking on the street in a rural district in Jamaica. John is heading in a northerly direction as he whimpers to himself about how bushy and thorny the countryside is. Everywhere he turns he sees only trees and stray animals competing with him for space. He needs to get to the corner grocer, but for him the distance is just too far and he continues to grumble about this too.

Jake on the other hand walking the same distance, needs to get to the drug store in close proximity to the corner grocer. As he passes the trees and the animals on the street he smiles to himself as he sees this as his opportunity to be one with nature. Even though the distance is quite a long way, he doesn't complain because he accepts it as his way of getting exercise since his schedule lately does not allow for this necessary routine. An added health benefit he muses.

There are times when I experience a downturn in business. Rather than complaining about my current circumstance, I take the opportunity to be thankful for all my blessings. I have so much to be grateful for.

Having a positive outlook doesn't mean being impractical. It doesn't mean that you are blinded to the realities of life, nor does it mean that you are living on another planet. What it does mean is that you are knowledgeable of all possible outcomes, but you choose to expect the best one will come your way, knowing that we attract that which we get. Choose to be positive.

The things we do, the goals we set and so on, are determined by the conversations we hold with our selves. Subsequently our environmental, financial, social and psychological statuses result from our habitual thinking. What are you telling yourself on a daily basis? A life of purpose does not self-sabotage. Many of us are unable to fulfill our destiny because of the lies we keep repeating to our selves. We continue to fail at everything we put our hands and hearts to and we can't seem to understand why. Many times when we don't get ahead we say it's because people don't like us. More often than not, the real reason lies in the fact that we are impairing or sabotaging our own self by speaking and thinking negatively about ourselves.

There is a direct correlation between our accomplishments or lack thereof and our way of thinking. For example, if you are working in a company and you get up every day thinking that the boss doesn't like you and that you are going to lose your job, then you probably will. Here's why: you will begin to underperform. In your head, it doesn't matter what you do, you won't find favour with your boss since he or she is out to get you. You begin to show up for work late and probably don't report to work on some days without even giving any notice. The company decides to downsize and so your employer has to make a decision about who to keep and who to let go. Certainly, any well thinking employer will have as their first choice those who have an excellent record of performance. Before you know it, you have talked yourself into losing your job all by your negative attitude and expectation.

The things we say to ourselves get lodged in our self-conscious and so we have to be resolute about depositing only positives. Believe that you deserve the best and will get the best. Believe that you deserve to have success and you will be successful. Stop doubting, start believing!

PERSEVERANCE

Success is never an overnight thing. If you fail at your first attempt, your best option is to try again. There are many examples of successful persons who at their first attempt did not succeed. Rather than giving up and indulging in self-pity, they kept going. One such example is McDonald's founder, Ray Kroc. At age fifty-two (52) Kroc was able to start a revolution in the franchise world. As a milk shake mixer salesman, he came across the McDonald brothers' (Richard and Maurice) hamburger shop in Southern California. They became Kroc's best customers purchasing his equipment as he struggled to keep his business going.

He investigated the McDonalds' business to ascertain why they were purchasing so many of his equipment. His expertise in the business led to the birth of the world renowned franchise with the bright yellow arches, after offering his services as their agent. The organization became the McDonald's Corporation after the opening of the first shop in 1955 in Chicago. A mere six years after, the McDonald brothers were bought out by Kroc. By 1965, there were more than seven hundred (700) sites in existence across the United States of America. Shortly thereafter, the franchise spread to several other countries and continues to spread across the globe.

Although the concept of the chain restaurant was not created by him, if Kroc had thought to himself that he was just a salesman and that he could not accomplish such a feat, the world would not have come to know what is undoubtedly the best when it comes on to systems that can be replicated so that quality is maintained throughout. What if at age 52, Kroc had thought to himself that he was too old to take on such a challenge?

Colonel Sanders of the world recognized Kentucky Fried Chicken (KFC) is another poignant example of the relentless pursuit of a dream. After retirement at age sixty-five (65) the Colonel began collecting his Social Security cheque of United States One Hundred Dollars (US$100.00). He wondered how he would survive financially. A great chef, he began to figure out a way to get his "secret recipe" across restaurants in the United States of America. He was laughed at and turned down on numerous occasions. After a little over one thousand (1,000) visits, he managed to finally convince Pete Harman in South Salt Lake, Utah to partner with him. They launched the first KFC site in 1952.

The KFC story is one of resilience and perseverance; reminding us not to give up on our dreams and aspirations regardless of how many negative responses we may receive.

We cannot speak of perseverance with mentioning Apple technology and Steve Jobs. Born to unwed graduate parents, he was given up for adoption at birth and only knew his biological parents when he was twenty-seven (27) years old. His unwavering commitment to the development of the Apple brand even when his team thought it could not be done was nothing short of phenomenal.

Lascelles Chin of the LASCO Group of Companies started out from humble beginnings. In his earlier days, he imported black pepper from the Far East and peas from Portugal and the United States. He wanted to expand his business and so turned to one of the major banks for a loan, which was subsequently denied. Later he partnered with the German firm, Henkel, where he was Chairman and Managing Director of the Jamaican arm. He was so successful in his tenure that he made Jamaica the highest per capita user of Henkel's adhesives in the world.

Chin now operates and manages several companies within the LASCO group. Distributing over 300 products worldwide, there is hardly a country anywhere in the world where you would not find a LASCO branded product.

The all important ingredients permeate all these stories— dedication, perseverance, and commitment.

GETTING (AND STAYING) MOTIVATED

Empowerment is critical. Living on purpose will force you to surround yourself with like-minded people to encourage and support you while avoiding those who are bringing you down. Identify from very early people with opportunistic and parasitic traits. Note that if someone is not with you, then he is against you; there is no middle ground. But rather than focusing your energies on such persons, focus on those who will mentor you into developing your full potential.

Even with the best intentions, getting up and doing the things we need to do to get ahead isn't always easy. Some of us form habits that are seemingly impossible to break and so we need an extra push to get us going. It is important to know that you are never alone in your struggle. Imagine motivation as the fuel in your motor vehicle. There is no way the car will run on E for too long; it will cover a short distance, but soon enough the petrol station which is just 5 minutes away will seem like years away if you don't have enough petrol to get you there.

Motivation is the petrol in our tank. Luckily, a refill is always available. There is an undeniable power in the written word for example. Books are invaluable to a mind that is intent on attaining excellence. Whenever you need an extra bout of motivation, read a good book. Zig Ziglar said, "Some people say motivation doesn't last, but neither does bathing; that's why we recommend it daily".

It is important to read about those who have gone ahead of you to learn from their experiences. Brandon Mull aptly puts it this way "Smart people learn from their mistakes but the real sharp ones learn from the mistakes of others." There is no need to reinvent the wheel; you will only be wasting precious time that could be used to sharpen your creative skills.

Pursuing your goal means that you will not allow your past to be a hindrance. Never mind the fact that you may not have the connection of colour or a surname that represents wealth; you were born with a brain which enables you to think. Deeply seated inside everyone, is the power of greatness. Never allow the world to be robbed of exposure to your leadership, skills and talents. You are more innovative, valuable and creative than you give yourself credit for. Let purpose be unleashed in you. There is always a way around the inevitable challenges. If you say you have no money, there are institutions that provide loans to start-ups; there are mentors willing and ready to provide guidance. Technology is literally at your fingertips to get the word out about your venture or learn new things. For example, you can learn any skill on YouTube.

Motivate yourself and allow the success of others to motivate you.

BEING A RIVER NOT A RESERVOIR

"The value of a man resides in what he gives and not in what he is capable of receiving."—Albert Einstein.

The biblical principle of giving has been proven time and again. When you give it will come back to you several times over. We should live our lives as rivers and not reservoirs. Let the blessing flow through you even as you have been richly blessed. Giving makes a difference especially when we see the difference it has made in the lives of others. To whom much is given, much is expected.

Just like a reservoir, we are not truly growing if we are not giving. There will only be some skills, talents and ideas welled up within us, looking for an escape valve. It is much better when we can liken our lives to a river with fresh water flowing through as it goes out.

We were all placed on this earth to serve others; if we all came to this realization there would be less poverty and less pain and more selfless acts of love and kindness. When we give, it not only benefits the recipients, it causes us to feel so much better and the more we give, the more we get.

It does not help when we are blessed and there are no beneficiaries of our blessing. There are several ways we can give back, such as mentoring someone in our field, monetary donation, free consultation, volunteering with organizations, etc. There is so much wealth of knowledge in this world; if we all do our part to pass on this knowledge the world would be an even greater place.

Many of us are talented leaders, mentors, advisors, and so on. In addition to our own growth and development, let's help others develop to their best selves too. There are many opportunities to share our gifts, skills and talents with others.

Make a resolve to volunteer with an organization that is aligned to your goals and vision. For example, I have committed to help spread the message of His Excellency The Most Honourable Sir Patrick Allen through his *"I Believe Initiative"*. This message resonates with me, "there is nothing wrong with Jamaica that cannot be fixed by what is right with Jamaica."

It helps too for us to constantly develop ourselves, learn new skills, and sharpen those we already have so that we can have so much more to offer to others.

RELIABILITY

A reliable person is capable of being depended upon.

How many times have you heard someone said, "I'll get back to you tomorrow," I'll deliver the package in two days," or "I'll send you a response by email in the next 30 minutes?" Somehow tomorrow never comes, two days turn into two weeks or another zero gets added to 30 minutes. If you have ever had to deal with people, then chances are you are very familiar with what I am talking about.

That so many people seem to be guilty of this is not an excuse to fall prey to the status quo. The only sure way to get ahead is to stand out. You can never stand out by being similar.

We should strive to keep our promises by doing what we said we would, in the time we promised to. If, for whatever reason you're unable to honour your commitment, say so the moment you recognize this and apologize for your delay.

Never neglect or shrug off your part; you will later regret this as people who are serious seek after like-minded individuals when they need things done.

Be consistently punctual; arrive when you say you would. If you have a tendency of being late, start to make amends by finding ways to remind you of what you need to do when you are supposed to, such as using the calendar on your phone and computer.

Be trustworthy, honest and steady in your business dealings; never give in to the temptation to be under-handed because you believe everyone is doing it.

Make a resolve to honour your word; let it be your bond. Sometimes after all is said and done, you only have your word to stand on. If you become known as someone who honours his word, in the rare occasion that you are unable to, people will be forgiving. If the reverse is true then you can never expect others to be sympathetic to your cause, as that is what they are accustomed to from you.

People who are serious about getting ahead are annoyed by unreliability. We do not live in a world where there is an ideal. There will always be unforeseen circumstances preventing you from honouring your word. However, the decent thing to do when these situations pop up is to give some heads up in advance of your stated deadline. Start by finding ways to manage yourself to spend the 24 hours in the day wisely.

This simple act can mean the difference between obtaining a contract or not.

SECTION II

CUSTOMER SERVICE

The sooner entrepreneurs realize the value of customer service, the quicker their businesses will begin to be seen as a serious contender for a sizeable share of their customers' wallets. We must know that it is by choice when customers spend their hard earned cash with us. They could easily go elsewhere. We need to honour the fact that they choose us and make their shopping experience more rewarding. Every customer or prospect, regardless of their mode of dress, colour, race, gender, age or other demographics should be treated with respect. A scene from the classic movie *Pretty Woman* starring Julia Roberts and Richard Gere is a poignant reminder. In the movie, Julia went to shop for clothes but because she was not dressed 'appropriately' the attendants would not wait on her.

The following day she got help from her "uncle" who accompanied her to another store where she shopped to her heart's content. When she was finished she went back to the first store and asked the unsuspecting assistant who had refused to wait on her whether she worked on commission. She did not recognize Julia as she was now dressed to fit the profile of what the store clerks were looking for. When she responded "yes," Julia, showing the many bags in her hand replied "big mistake, you wouldn't wait on me yesterday" and then walked out of the store, much to the attendant's dismay.

Bringing this example to reality, billionaire Oprah Winfrey's request to see a handbag in a Swiss store was refused because the sales clerk thought she would not be able to afford it. The sad reality is that Winfrey was profiled as unable to afford an expensive purse no doubt because of her skin colour. If only the sales agent had known who Oprah Winfrey was! The moral of the story is not to judge a person's spending capacity based on any physical appearance or dress. It reminds us to treat everyone with respect as their outward appearance does not determine the power of their wallet or anything else about them expect what is visible at that time.

The customers' interest must be placed at heart at all times; it is important to get to know them, to let them feel part of the business. They need to know that they are valuable to the business and it was not that one purchase that you are after.

Be humble in your interactions with everyone. Pride goes before a fall. Some persons were born into fame while others have fame bestowed upon them. Whatever or however you've received your fame, it is important to remember to be humble. Resist the temptation to see yourself superior to other human beings. All men have been created equal.

Patwa Apparel has fourteen (14) points of culture or core values that we operate on. Customer Service ranks very high on that list. The comments made by customers in our guest book speak volumes to this fact; likewise the reviews made by visitors on the travel website, *tripadvisor.com*.

MARKETING

Marketing is yet another entrepreneurial life blood. It is simply that critical business function that is responsible for attracting, retaining and growing customers. Or put another way, the art of getting the word out about your product is marketing or branding. No one will be able to support your business if they are unaware of its existence.

A brand is a symbol, name, design or anything that differentiates your product from the competition. The term branding has its genesis in a time when cattle owners would literally place a mark on their animals by 'branding' with a hot iron which would leave an imprint on the animal. This is no different in modern times, where brand owners use a mark that is easily distinguishable from similar products on the market.

As the battle intensifies to get and keep customers, it is important that you take the time to research, define and build your brand. Once that is done, then there needs to be a strategy to make buyers aware of your existence so that you will be able to have a share of what is in their wallet.

Some important points for consideration are:

Product: There must be a product or service that customers are willing to let go of their hard earned cash for. It should not be the same as what the competitor next door is offering. Some important questions need to be answered. What is your guarantee that your product or service is different? Why should a consumer purchase your product over the competitor's? Customers have a problem to solve and your product/service must be the solution.

Promotion: This aspect has to do with how the information about your offering will be communicated? How will your target market know that you exist? Whilst today's technological environment makes it easier than say, 10 years ago to promote your product/ service on the internet and social media, the competition for the customer's attention also intensifies. This means that your information must get out in the shortest possible time given the decreasingly short attention span of those you are targeting.

Price: What will be your price point; low, mid or high? This will be determined by a number of factors such as competitors' price, market value, cost of inputs, profit margin, and so forth.

Place: Location is everything. It is imperative that your target market will be able to locate your business without any hassle. Where you are located will be dependent upon first and foremost the market you are targeting, affordability, proximity to amenities, etc.

Operating on a shoe string budget does not allow for huge marketing campaigns, however, there must be a clear strategy to communicate the existence of your business' products and services. There is no denying that advertising in the mainstream media is costly.

Although marketing is an investment, it is not an investment that most start-ups and MSMEs can readily afford to make in the early stages of business. Still, it is imperative that you find an avenue to properly market your goods or service. Business persons in this era have so much advantage over their forerunners. To start, the access to social media literally at your fingertips is more than any business savvy individual could ever ask for. By the click of a button with e-marketing software thousands of customers and prospects can be reached at any one time.

There is no excuse for your target market to be unaware of your product or service. Google Plus, Twitter, Facebook and a host of others create an inexpensive platform for market awareness and penetration. Youtube provides an excellent medium for others to literally see what you have to offer.

Consumers don't like to buy products in a vacuum, they like to know that they know, or at least know about the owner. It makes them more comfortable and safe. In promoting your product, you will have to promote yourself; don't be bashful about this. There is no shame where business is concerned. Go after what you want. Part of what you want is to be profitable. It is interesting to find that many business persons are uncomfortable with networking. News flash, your network is your net worth. How much you are worth in business depends on how many people you know and who know you. It sounds simple but people are more comfortable doing business with people they know or at least know something about. Business is greatly about relationship.

One of the quickest ways to get people to know about you and your products is to attend events and issue business cards. If you attend an event in your field ask whether there is a mailing list and ask to be put on it. In turn, please collect business cards and send follow up emails soon after you have left the event. You will be kept fresh in the minds of those prospects. Create a database and ensure you keep in contact at least once per quarter or if necessary, once per month. You are sending a subliminal message about your business—this is very important especially in a time when what is to our advantage is also a disadvantage. The easy access to technology means that the market place is constantly noisy. We have to be purposeful in getting the attention of those we are targeting, but it can be done.

Blogging is also another way to promote yourself and your business. Again, this is an area in which there are several platforms to do this. Write stories that are related to your field or just about anything that you believe your target market will want to read about. Google's platform, *Blogger* is available free to anyone wanting to start a blog. The templates are quite user friendly too. In addition to *Blogger*, there are several other options available.

In addition to the aforementioned points, it is important to consider that what you are presenting to the customer is always clean, crisp and professional. This includes your storefront, merchandise and marketing material such as flyers, business cards and brochures.

As a business owner you should try being different and extraordinary, a guaranteed way to experience success.

Get into the habit of practicing being nice to everyone, including those who did not buy from you. Always have an attitude of service approach.

There is no such thing as a detached business owner. Those who are successful in business do so with passion and spirit. Part of demonstrating your passion is the ability to network with others and sharing your business. Networking benefits all those within your circle. It not only helps you to get business and increase your revenue, it helps you to strengthen your supply chain by identifying persons who provide goods and services which you have a need for at some point in the future.

Have a heart and spirit for what you do and the excitement will catch on. Be you, be real. If it doesn't feel right; don't do it.

FINANCIALS

It is important to have accurate and timely financials to run your business effectively. Many business owners especially small business owners do not take the time necessary to ensure their financials are kept impeccably updated. They are so busy carrying out the everyday functions they neglect to keep check of their numbers.

Financial statements not only tell you the value and performance of your business, they also help you manage your company when you can no longer be hands on with all the details. It is also what others use to measure your company. For example when you go to the bank for a loan for your business, bankers use your Income and Cash Flow Statements and Balance Sheets to determine the health of your business.

The Income Statement shows the revenue earned and related expenses over a given period, say a fiscal year. It is designed to determine whether you made a profit.

The Balance Sheet gives you a picture of your assets and liabilities over a period.

The Cash Flow Statement reconciles the net profit from the Income Statement to the amount of cash generated for that same period.

It is critical to get your financials in order form the onset of your business. It is quite fine to start with an Excel spreadsheet outlining income and expenditure. As the business begins to grow user-friendly software such as **Quickbooks** is a viable option.

Still, as your business grows further, employ the service of a full time accountant and rid yourself of what can be a burden if this is not your area of expertise. If you decide to source the help of a professional, choose very carefully. This will spare you a world of uneasiness. From my experience, it would be wise for you to always stay on top of your Accountant's work. Even though he or she is the expert with the numbers, you know your business best. It is important to have an idea of what to do so that you will know whether your Accountant is posting entries correctly to generate your figures. This is key as "garbage in, garbage out" is applicable not just to the field of technology, but in all spheres of life.

File your tax returns with the statutory bodies as soon as they become due. Some persons are afraid of keeping proper records and paying taxes. However, the pros of doing this far outweigh the cons. For example, obtaining grant funding and loans will require that your books are up to date and that you are tax compliant. The added benefit of peace of mind is worth any trouble you go through doing this. Get this out of the way from early on.

As a small business owner, you will find that you may file your monthly returns, but you may need to employ an accountant to do your annual returns. If your business is registered as a company, surely you will need audited financial reports at the end of your financial year.

INTELLECTUAL PROPERTY

Intellectual Property is a creation of the mind for which sole rights are recognized and attributed to the creator or developer of such ideas. Intellectual Property (IP) refers to any creation involving the mind relating to symbols, names, images, designs, invention, literary and artistic works for the purpose of commerce and trade. They can either be industrial or copyright. Industrial IP refers to trademarks, inventions (patents), industrial designs or geographic indications.

Copyright involves literary works such as films, books, traditional knowledge, poems and artistic works such as painting and drawings.

A patent in an exclusive right granted for an invention. A patent gives the owner the right to decide whether or how the invention may be used by others. The patent owner usually makes technical information about the invention available to the public in published patent documents.

Looking specifically at Trademarks:

A trademark is any sign or symbol which distinguishes your goods and services from another person's, for example, words, logos, pictures or any combination of these. They serve as a marketing tool to help your target market recognize your product or service while helping to build the strength of your brand.

When contemplating registering your trademark, you need to consider its distinctiveness; it should not look similar to existing marks otherwise you may not be able to register it with your IP office. There are some slogans or marks that are trade jargons for example 'tasty food' which is simply a description for any food category and so you will not be able to claim rights of usage.

Marks are registered for a period of ten (10) years after which they should be renewed to show that the mark is still being used. If the mark is being used outside of your territory/country, usually by about year three (3) you will need to prove that the mark is being used for it to maintain its validity.

The registration process is quite simple whether you are doing it in Jamaica, the USA or in the European territories. For example, in Europe you may register your mark in several countries at once using the Community Trademark (CTM). The Madrid Protocol is also another option for registering your mark internationally. Jamaica is advanced in its discussion to becoming a signatory to this protocol which will make it much easier for persons wanting international protection of their mark.

Another important aspect to consider is the class or category where you want to register your mark. The option to register in more than one class is available. Protecting your IP is an investment. If at the onset you are unable to afford the registration with your IP office, the lay man's option is available to show proof of ownership. To do this, seal the mark in an envelope and visit your local post office to register the mail to yourself. This should remain unopened until in the event a dispute arises where you will need to show as proof, the mark belongs to you.

NEGOTIATION

Negotiation is a must in any business. This is simply interactive communication that takes place whenever we want something from someone or when someone wants something from us. It is a dialogue (not a monologue) to find a fair compromise for the parties involved. Another term for negotiation is simply bargaining.

Negotiation is never a one-time thing. It begins from the first impression you make the moment you meet a new contact and follows through to the moment the deal is signed off on.

Some factors affecting negotiations are language, customs, social expectations and religion.

Some questions to ask going into any form of negotiation are:

a. What is it that you want to get from this deal and what is it that you think the other party wants?
b. What do you and the other person have that you can trade?
c. What do you each have that the other wants?
d. What are you each comfortable giving away?
e. If you don't reach an agreement with the other person, what alternatives do you have?
f. What are the consequences of winning or losing both for you and the other party?
g. What possible outcomes might there be?

Whatever the circumstance, when doing any form of business negotiation, remember the following points:

1. Do not get personal; instead stick to the business facts.
2. Check your emotional temperature and resist the temptation to get overheated if the discussions are not going in your favour.
3. Do not talk out of school; let the matters discussed remain between the parties.
4. Both sides must win something otherwise there can't be a favourable deal.
5. Never make your first offer your final offer.
6. Do not negotiate with yourself; wait for the other party to make a counter offer before placing another offer on the table.
7. Never be too risk-averse; business is about taking risks.
8. If it appears that you are in over your head seek expert advise
9. You may be able to get what you want by calling it another name.
10. Importantly, take your time to come to a decision.

In order to succeed in any business venture, we must carefully master the art of getting our desired outcome while at the same time ensuring that there is something in the deal for the other party. Entrepreneurs must negotiate strategically, knowing how to operate across various boundaries such as race, culture, gender, age and all other demographics.

Proper planning is important. Consider how much time you will have to present your case and prepare your agenda based on that.

We must never attempt to win it all to the expense of the person with whom we are negotiating. Do this and you are sure to have them walk away with a bitter taste in their mouths. Long after the negotiation, the parties will need to be able to trust each other; a selfish negotiation will erode the possibility for this to happen. Mutual trust leads to a positive relationship.

A positive relationship makes possible a common ground with similar goals and objectives to the point where there is shared interest.

In order for it to be a win-win, both parties must feel positive once the negotiation is over. This will be important for a good working relationship afterwards. This is critical as a high percentage of business is about relationship. We should always place a high premium on maintaining good, professional working relationships with those with whom we do business.

Especially in this technologically advanced age, the world is a much smaller place than it used to be. This is great, but it also places greater pressure on us to be professional. You don't want to treat someone poorly and find that you have to come in contact with them another year from now in another capacity. The basic rule of thumb is to treat people the way you want to be treated.

Resolve to be a skilled negotiator and you are well on your way to entrepreneurial success. It takes practice. Each time you negotiate with someone, make an evaluation of your performance; keep doing the things that were done right and seek to improve upon those areas where you were weak. If you attended a meeting with a partner, ask him or her to make an assessment of the things you did as there is always room for improvement. Accept criticisms in the manner they were meant; don't take them personally.

PLANNING

Planning is simply a process where we think about and organize the necessary activities required to achieve a desired objective or goal. There can be no success without this necessary criterion. Careful planning is important whether we are managing a church, a home, a major project or just simply doing routine chores.

I have found the times when I was least successful in my life in general and my business ventures in particular, were the times when I never had a carefully thought out plan. It made a vast difference the moment I developed a plan and stuck with it.

In his words of wisdom, Zig Ziglar left this thought with us, "you were born to win, but to be a winner, you must PLAN (emphasis added) to win, prepare to win and expect to win".

"If you fail to plan then you should plan to fail." No doubt this has been said over and again and it is by no means a mere cliché. This is all so critical to managing a business. Banks and other funding agencies invariably want to see evidence of a careful plan for your business before they hand you their money. Whether you are a start-up or a business with many years under your belt, you will need this guide to access loans, grants or simply to experience business growth.

Even if you decide against loans, it is always best to strategically write your plan down for your own assessment of where you are currently and where you need to be. Whatever your reason for the plan, ensure it is well written (a template is included in the appendices).

It cannot be emphasized enough that you will not be success without having a plan; it's a major key to success.

* * *

Nothing in life that is worth having comes easy. Among other things, it will take commitment, hard work, a sense of purpose and perseverance to succeed. We must be resolute about accomplishing our goals. I charge that you will commit to the cause in the pursuit of your goals in whatever sphere of life that you choose. I leave with you a quote from Henry Wadsworth Longfellow—"The heights of great men reached and kept, were not attained by sudden flight; but they while their companions slept, were toiling upwards through the night."

Live purposefully on purpose!

APPENDIX

The Business Plan

Below is a template to help you get started. This was gleaned from the website www.business.gov.au and amended to reflect the Jamaican environment:

Using this template

Before you complete this business plan template and start using it, consider the following:

Do your research. You will need to make quite a few decisions about your business including structure, marketing strategies and finances before you can complete the template. By having the right information at hand you will also be more accurate in your forecasts and analysis.

Determine who the plan is for. Does it have more than one purpose? Will it be used internally or will third parties be involved? Deciding the purpose of the plan can help you target your answers. If third parties are involved, what are they interested in? Although, don't assume they are just interested in the finance part of your business. They will be looking for the whole package.

Do not attempt to fill in the template from start to finish. First decide which sections are relevant for your business and set aside the sections that don't apply. You can always go back to the other sections later.

Use the [*italicized text*]. The italicized text is there to help guide you by providing some more detailed questions you may like to answer when preparing your response. ***Please note:*** If a question does not apply to your circumstances it can be ignored.

Get some help. If you aren't confident in completing the plan yourself, you can enlist the help of a professional (i.e. Business Support Organizations such as JAMPRO, JBDC, business adviser, or accountant) to look through your plan and provide you with advice.

Actual vs. expected figures. Existing businesses can include actual figures in the plan, but if your business is just starting out or about to start and you are using expected figures for turnover and finances, you will need to clearly show that these are expected figures or estimates.

Write your summary last. Use as few words as possible. You want to get to the point but not overlook important facts. This is also your opportunity to sell yourself. But don't overdo it. You want prospective banks, investors, partners or wholesalers to be able to quickly read your plan, find it realistic and be motivated by what they read.

Review. Review. Review. Your business plan is there to make a good impression. Errors will only detract from your professional image. So ask a number of impartial people to proofread your final plan.

[INSERT YOUR BUSINESS LOGO]

[Your Name]
[Your Title]
[Business Name]
[Main Business Address]

[Business Name]

Business Plan

Prepared: *[Date prepared]*

Business Plan Summary

[*Please complete this page last*]

[*Your business summary should be no longer than a page and should focus on why your business is going to be successful. Your answers below should briefly summarize your more detailed answers provided throughout the body of this plan.*]

The Business

Business name: [*Enter your business name as registered in your territory. If you have not registered your business name, add your proposed business name.*]

Business structure: [*Sole trader, partnership, trust, company.*]

Business location: [*Main business location*]

Date established: [*The date you started trading.*]

Business owner(s): [*List all of the business owners.*]

Relevant owner experience:[*Briefly outline your experience and/or years in the industry and any major achievements/awards.*]

Products/services:[*What products/services are you selling? What is the anticipated demand for your products/services?*]

The Market

Target market:

[*Who are you selling to? Why would they buy your products/services over others?*]

Marketing strategy:

[*How do you plan to enter the market? How do you intend to attract customers? How and why will this work?*]

The Future

Vision statement:

[*The vision statement briefly outlines your future plan for the business. It should state clearly what your overall goals for the business are.*]

Goals/objectives:

[*What are your short & long term goals? What activities will you undertake to meet them?*]

The Finances

[*Briefly outline how much profit you intend on making in a particular timeframe. How much money will you need up-front? Where will you obtain these funds? What portion will you be seeking from other sources? How much of your own money are you contributing towards the business?*]

The Business

Business details

Products/services:[*What products/services are you selling? What is the anticipated demand for your products/services?*]

Registration details

Business name: [*Enter your business name as registered in your state/territory. If you have not registered your business name, add your proposed business name.*]

Trading name(s): [*Registered trading name(s).*]

Date registered: [*Date business name registered.*]

Location(s) registered:[*State(s) you are registered in.*]

Business structure:[*Sole trader, partnership, trust, company.*]

Domain names:[*Registered domain names.*]

Licenses & permits: [*List all the licenses or permits you have registered*]

Business premises

Business location: [*Describe the location and space occupied/ required. What is the size of the space you occupy/require? Which city or town? Where in relation to landmarks/main areas? If you have a retail business, where are you in relation to other shops? What is the retail traffic like?*]

Buy/lease: [*If you have purchased a business premises or are currently leasing, briefly outline the arrangements. If you are still looking for a lease, outline your commercial lease requirements and any utilities/facilities required.*]

Organization chart

[*Outline your business structure in the chart below.*]

Figure 1: Organisation Chart. [Complete this chart or include your own.]

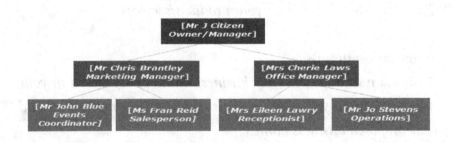

Management & ownership

Names of owners:[*List all of the business owners.*]

Details of management & ownership: [*As the owner(s), will you be running the business or will a Chief Executive Officer (CEO) be*] *running the business on your behalf? What will be your involvement? If it is a partnership briefly outline % share, role in the business, the strengths of each partner and whether you have a partnership agreement/contract in place?]*

Experience: *[What experience do the business owner(s) have? How many years have you owned or run a business? List any previous businesses owned/managed. List any major achievements/awards. What other relevant experience do you have? Don't forget to attach your resume(s) to the back of your plan.]*

Key personnel

Current staff
[List your current staff in the table below.]

Job Title	Name	Expected staff turnover	Skills or strengths
[e.g. Marketing/ Sales Manager]	*[Mr Chris Brantley]*	*[12-18 months]*	*[Relevant qualifications in Sales/ Marketing. At least 5 years experience in the industry. Award in marketing excellence.]*
[e.g. Marketing/ Sales Manager]	*[Mr Chris Brantley]*	*[12-18 months]*	*[Relevant qualifications in Sales/ Marketing. At least 5 years experience in the industry. Award in marketing excellence.]*
[e.g. Marketing/ Sales Manager]	*[Mr Chris Brantley]*	*[12-18 months]*	*[Relevant qualifications in Sales/ Marketing. At least 5 years experience in the industry. Award in marketing excellence.]*

Job Title	Name	Expected staff turnover	Skills or strengths
[e.g. Marketing/ Sales Manager]	*[Mr Chris Brantley]*	*[12-18 months]*	*[Relevant qualifications in Sales/ Marketing. At least 5 years experience in the industry. Award in marketing excellence.]*

Required staff

[List your required staff in the table below.]

Job Title	Quantity	Expected staff turnover	Skills necessary	Date required
[e.g. Office Manager]	*[1]*	*[2-3 years]*	*[Relevant qualifications in Office Management. At least 2 years experience.]*	*[Month/ Year]*
[e.g. Office Manager]	*[1]*	*[2-3 years]*	*[Relevant qualifications in Office Management. At least 2 years experience.]*	*[Month/ Year]*
[e.g. Office Manager]	*[1]*	*[2-3 years]*	*[Relevant qualifications in Office Management. At least 2 years experience.]*	*[Month/ Year]*
[e.g. Office Manager]	*[1]*	*[2-3 years]*	*[Relevant qualifications in Office Management. At least 2 years experience.]*	*[Month/ Year]*

Recruitment options

[How do you intend on obtaining your required staff? Advertising in the local paper, online advertising, and/or training current staff members?]

Training programs

[Are there any training programs you will be organising in the event you cannot find the required skills? Are these in-house or external providers? What training will you as the business owner/manager undertake to keep your skills current?]

Skill retention strategies

[What procedural documentation will you provide to ensure the skills of staff are maintained? Do you have an appropriate allocation of responsibilities? How are responsibilities documented and communicated to staff? What internal processes will you implement to regularly check that the current skills of staff members are still appropriate for the business?]

Products/services

Product/Service	Description	Price
[Product/service name]	*[Brief product/service description]*	*[Price including GCT]*
[Product/service name]	*[Brief product/service description]*	*[Price including GCT]*
[Product/service name]	*[Brief product/service description]*	*[Price including GCT]*
[Product/service name]	*[Brief product/service description]*	*[Price including GCT]*

Market position: *[Where do your products/services fit in the market? Are they high-end, competitive or budget? How does this compare to your competitors?]*

Unique selling position: *[How will your products/services succeed in the market where others may have failed? What gives your products/services the edge?]*

Anticipated demand: [*What is the anticipated quantity of products/ services your customers are likely to purchase? For example, how much will an individual customer buy in 6 months or 12 months?*]

Pricing strategy: [*Do you have a particular pricing strategy? Why have you chosen this strategy?*]

Value to customer: [*How do your customers view your products/ services? Are they a necessity, luxury or something in between?*]

Growth potential: [*What is the anticipated percentage growth of the product in the future? What will drive this growth?*]

Innovation

Research & development (R&D)/innovation activities

[*What R&D activities will you implement to encourage innovation in your business? What financial and/or staff resources will you allocate?*]

Intellectual property strategy

[*How do you plan to protect your innovations? List any current trademarks, patents, designs you have registered. Do you have confidentiality agreements in place?*]

Risk management

[List the potential risks (in order of likelihood) that could impact your business.]

Risk	Likelihood	Impact	Strategy
[Description of the risk and the potential impact to your business.]	[Highly Unlikely, Unlikely, Likely, Highly Likely]	[High, Medium, Low]	[What actions will you take to minimise/ mitigate the potential risk to your business?]
[Description of the risk and the potential impact to your business.]	[Highly Unlikely, Unlikely, Likely, Highly Likely]	[High, Medium, Low]	[What actions will you take to minimize/mitigate the potential risk to your business?]

Legal considerations

[List the legislation which will have some impact on the running of your business. For example: consumer law, business law, or specific legislation to your industry.]

Operations

Production process

[What is the process involved in producing your products or services. This process will vary depending on your product or service. Here are some examples of questions you may consider. Is there a manufacturing process? Who is involved in the process? Are there any third parties involved? What is involved in delivering the service to your customers?]

Suppliers

[Who are your main suppliers? What do they supply to your business? How will you maintain a good relationship with them?]

Plant & equipment

[List your current plant and equipment purchases. These can include vehicles, computer equipment, phones and fax machines.]

Equipment	Purchase date	Purchase price	Running cost
[e.g Personal Computer]	*[eg. 20/03/2010]*	*[e.g $2100]*	*[e.g $100 a month]*
[e.g Personal Computer]	*[eg. 20/03/2010]*	*[e.g $2100]*	*[e.g $100 a month]*
[e.g Personal Computer]	*[eg. 20/03/2010]*	*[e.g $2100]*	*[e.g $100 a month]*
[e.g Personal Computer]	*[eg. 20/03/2010]*	*[e.g $2100]*	*[e.g $100 a month]*

Inventory

[List your current inventory items in the table below. If you have a substantial inventory, you may prefer to attach a full inventory list to the back of this business plan.]

Inventory item	Unit price	Quantity in stock	Total cost
[e.g flour]	*[e.g $5.00kg]*	*[e.g Five kilograms]*	*[e.g $25.00]*
[e.g flour]	*[e.g $5.00kg]*	*[e.g Five kilograms]*	*[e.g $25.00]*
[e.g flour]	*[e.g $5.00kg]*	*[e.g Five kilograms]*	*[e.g $25.00]*
[e.g flour]	*[e.g $5.00kg]*	*[e.g Five kilograms]*	*[e.g $25.00]*

Technology (Software): *[What technology do you require? For example: website, point of sale software or accounting package? What will be the main purpose for each? Will they be off-the-shelf or purpose built? What is the estimated cost of each technology solution?]*

Trading hours: [*What are your trading hours? What are your expected peak trading times? Which times do you expect to be more profitable? How will this change over different seasons? How do your trading hours accommodate these changes?*]

Communication channels: [*How can your customers get in contact with you? These channels can include: telephone (landline/ mobile), post box, shopfront, email, fax, internet blog or social media channel.*]

Payment types accepted: [*What payment types will you accept. cash, credit, cheque, gift cards, Paypal, etc*]

Credit policy: [*What is your credit policy for customers/suppliers? How long is the credit period? What are your collection strategies/ procedures? What credit does your business receive? What are the terms?*]

Warranties & refunds: [*If you manufacture certain goods, what are the warranty terms? What is your business refund/exchange policy?*]

Quality control:[*Describe your quality control process. What checks or balances do you have in place to ensure the product or service you offer is produced to the same standard of quality? What steps do you take to meet product safety standards?*]

Memberships & affiliations:[*Is your business a member of any particular industry association or club? Do you have any affiliations with any other organization?*]

Sustainability plan

Environmental/resource impacts
[*Describe the impact your business could potentially have on the environment. E.g. a particular manufacturing process may contribute negatively on the local water supply.*]

Community impact & engagement
[*How does your environment impact/affect the local community? How can you engage the community in minimizing your impact?*]

Risks/constraints
[*List any risks/constraints to your business resulting from this environmental impact?*]

Strategies
[*What strategies will you implement to minimize/mitigate your environmental impact and any risks to your business? Will you conduct an environmental audit? Have you introduced an Environmental management system?*]

Action plan
[*List your key sustainability/environmental milestones below?*]

Sustainability milestone	Target	Target date
[*Reduce water consumption*]	[*60% reduction*]	[*Month/Year*]
[*Reduce water consumption*]	[*60% reduction*]	[*Month/Year*]
[*Reduce water consumption*]	[*60% reduction*]	[*Month/Year*]

The Market

Market research
[*What statistical research have you completed to help you analyze your market? Did you use a survey/questionnaire? If so, you may like to attach a copy of your survey/questionnaire to the back of this plan.*]

Market targets
[*Outline your planned sales targets. What quantity of your products/ services do you plan to sell in a planned timeframe? Are they monthly or yearly targets?*]

Environmental/industry analysis
[*Detail the results of the market research you have performed. Is the area experiencing population growth? Are there long-term employers in the area? Is the region's economy stable? Are there seasonal variations?*

What is the size of the market? What recent trends have emerged in the market? What growth potential is available and where do you fit in? How will the market/customers change when you enter the market?]

Your customers

Customer demographics
[*Define who your target customers are and how they behave. You can include age, gender, social status, education and attitudes.*]

Key customers

[*Identify your key customers. (These can be large consumers of your products or individuals whose satisfaction is key to the success of your business.) How will you target your products/service to them?*]

Customer management

[*How will you maintain a good relationship with your customers? What techniques will you use? How will you keep your customers coming back? Have you introduced customer service standards? Do you follow any particular code of practice?*]

S.W.O.T. analysis

[*List each of your businesses strengths, weaknesses, opportunities or threats in the table below and then outline how you plan to address each of the weaknesses/threats.*]

Strengths	Weaknesses
[*e.g High traffic location*]	[*e.g High rental costs*]
Opportunities	**Threats**
[*e.g build on customer and brand loyalty*]	[*e.g Cash flow problems*]

Your competitors

[*How do you rate against your competitors? How can your business improve on what they offer?*]

Competitor details

List at least 5 competitors stating their name, where and when they were established, estimated percent of market share, unique value to customers and competitors main weakness.

Advertising & sales

Advertising & promotional strategy

[What strategies do you have for promoting and advertising your products/services in the next 12 months?]

Planned promotion / advertising type	Expected business improvement	Cost ($)	Target date
[Print media advertising, online advertising, mail-out, giveaway, media release, social media campaign or event.]	[How do you expect it will improve your business success?]	[$]	[Month/Year]
[Print media advertising, online advertising, mail-out, giveaway, media release, social media campaign or event.]	[How do you expect it will improve your business success?]	[$]	[Month/Year]
[Print media advertising, online advertising, mail-out, giveaway, media release, social media campaign or event.]	[How do you expect it will improve your business success?]	[$]	[Month/Year]
[Print media advertising, online advertising, mail-out, giveaway, media release, social media campaign or event.]	[How do you expect it will improve your business success?]	[$]	[Month/Year]

Sales & marketing objectives

[Who makes up your sales team? What sales techniques will they use? What tools/material will they use to help sell your products/ services? What sales goals/targets will they meet?]

Unique selling position

[*Why do you have an advantage over your competitors? How will your products/services succeed in the market where others may have failed?*]

Sales & distribution channels

Channel type	Products/ services	Sales (%)	Pros	Cons
[*e.g. Shopfront, internet, direct mail, export or wholesale*]	[*List all the products/ services sold via this channel*]	[*What percentage of overall sales do you expect to sell via this channel?*]	[*What advantages are there of using this channel for these products?*]	[*What challenges do you expect to face using this channel? How will you overcome them?*]
[*e.g. Shopfront, internet, direct mail, export or wholesale*]	[*List all the products/ services sold via this channel*]	[*What percentage of overall sales do you expect to sell via this channel?*]	[*What advantages are there of using this channel for these products?*]	[*What challenges do you expect to face using this channel? How will you overcome them?*]

The Future

Vision statement

[*What is your business' vision statement? It should briefly outline your future plan for the business and include your overall goals.*]

Mission statement

[*What is your business' mission statement? I.e. how will you achieve your vision?*]

Goals/objectives

[What are your short & long term goals? What activities will you undertake to meet them?]

Action plan

Please note: This table does not include sustainability milestones as they are listed in the sustainability section above.

Milestone	Date of expected completion	Person responsible
[What are the business milestones that you need to complete starting from today?]	*[When do you expect to complete them?]*	*[Who is responsible for delivering this milestone?]*
[What are the business milestones that you need to complete starting from today?]	*[When do you expect to complete them?]*	*[Who is responsible for delivering this milestone?]*
[What are the business milestones that you need to complete starting from today?]	*[When do you expect to complete them?]*	*[Who is responsible for delivering this milestone?]*

The Finances

Key objectives & financial review

Financial objectives

[List your key financial objectives. These can be in the form of sales or profit targets. You could also list your main financial management goals such as cost reduction targets.]

Finance required

[How much money up-front do you need? Where will you obtain the funds? What portion will you be seeking from loans, investors, business partners, friends or relatives, venture capital or government

funding? How much of your own money are you contributing towards the business?]

Assumptions

The financial tables on the subsequent pages are based on the assumptions listed below:

[List your financial assumptions. These can include seasonal adjustments, drought or interest rates etc.]

Start-up costs for [YEAR]

[Consider the information below when developing your own start up costing sheet to include in your business plan.]

START-UP COSTS	Cost ($)	EQUIPMENT/CAPITAL COSTS	Cost ($)
Registrations		Business purchase price	
Business name		Franchise fees	
Licences		Start-up capital	
Permits		**Plant & equipment**	
Domain names		Vehicles	
Trade marks/designs/patents		Computer equipment	
Vehicle registration		Computer software	
More...		Phones	
Membership fees		Fax machine	
Accountant fees		More...	
Solicitor fees		Security system	
Rental lease cost (Rent advance/deposit)		**Office equipment**	
Utility connections & bonds (Electricity, gas, water)		Furniture	
Phone connection		Shop fitout	
Internet connection		More...	
Computer software			
Training			
Wages			
Stock/raw materials			
Insurance			
Building & contents			
Vehicle			
Public liability			
Professional indemnity			
Product liability			
Workers compensation			
Business assets			
Business revenue			
Printing			
Stationery & office supplies			
Marketing & advertising			
More...			
Total start-up costs	$0	**Total equipment/capital costs**	$0

Balance sheet forecast

[Consider the information below when developing your own Balance sheet forecast to include in your business plan.]

BALANCE SHEET FORECAST	[Year 1]	[Year 2]	[Year 3]
Current assets			
Cash			
Petty cash			
Inventory			
Pre-paid expenses			
Fixed assets			
Leasehold			
Property & land			
Renovations/improvements			
Furniture & fitout			
Vehicles			
Equipment/tools			
Computer equipment			
More...			
Total assets	$0	$0	$0
Current/short-term liabilities			
Credit cards payable			
Accounts payable			
Interest payable			
Accrued wages			
Income tax			
More...			
Long-term liabilities			
Loans			
More...			
Total liabilities	$0	$0	$0
NET ASSETS	$0	$0	$0

Profit and loss forecast

[Consider the information below when developing your own profit & loss sheet to include in your business plan.]

PROFIT & LOSS FORECAST	[Year 1]	[Year 2]	[Year 3]
Sales			
less cost of goods sold			
More...			
Gross profit/net sales	$0	$0	$0
Expenses			
Accountant fees			
Advertising & marketing			
Bank fees & charges			
Bank interest			
Credit card fees			
Utilities (electricity, gas, water)			
Telephone			
Lease/loan payments			
Rent & rates			
Motor vehicle expenses			
Repairs & maintenance			
Stationery & printing			
Insurance			
Superannuation			
Income tax			
Wages (including PAYG)			
More...			
Total expenses	$0	$0	$0
NET PROFIT	$0	$0	$0

Expected cash flow

[Consider the information below when developing your own expected cash flow sheet to include in your business plan.]

EXPECTED CASHFLOW [YEAR]	Jan	Feb	Mar	Apr	May	Jun	Jul	Aug	Sep	Oct	Nov	Dec
OPENING BALANCE	$0	$0	$0	$0	$0	$0	$0	$0	$0	$0	$0	$0
Cash incoming												
Sales												
Asset sales												
Debtor receipts												
Other income												
Total incoming	$0	$0	$0	$0	$0	$0	$0	$0	$0	$0	$0	$0
Cash outgoing												
Purchases (Stock etc)												
Accountant fees												
Solicitor fees												
Advertising & marketing												
Bank fees & charges												
Interest paid												
Credit card fees												
Utilities (electricity, gas, water)												
Telephone												
Lease/loan payments												
Rent & rates												
Motor vehicle expenses												
Repairs & maintenance												
Stationery & printing												
Membership & affiliation fees												
Licensing												
Insurance												
Superannuation												
Income tax												
Wages (including PAYG)												
More...												
Total outgoing	$0	$0	$0	$0	$0	$0	$0	$0	$0	$0	$0	$0
Monthly cash balance	$0	$0	$0	$0	$0	$0	$0	$0	$0	$0	$0	$0
CLOSING BALANCE	$0	$0	$0	$0	$0	$0	$0	$0	$0	$0	$0	$0

Break-even analysis

[Consider the information below when performing your own break-even analysis.]

BREAK-EVEN CALCULATOR	
Timeframe (e.g. monthly/yearly)	
Average price of each product/service sold	
Average cost of each product/service to make/deliver	
Fixed costs for the month/year	
Percentage of price that is profit	
Total sales needed to break-even	
Number of units sold needed to break-even	

Supporting documentation

Attached is my supporting documentation in relation to this business plan. The attached documents include:

[List all of your attachments here. These may include resumes, inventory list, survey/questionnaire and/or financial documents.].

IMPORTANT AGENCY CONTACTS

Companies Office of Jamaica
1 Grenada Way
Kingston 5
Email: custsupport@orcjamaica.com
Website: www.orcjamaica.com
Telephone # 908-4419-26

Tax Administration Services Department
Taxpayer Registration Centre
12 Ocean Boulevard
Kingston Mall, Kingston
Website: www.jamaicatax.gov.jm
Telephone #969-0000-7

JAMPRO
18 Trafalgar Road
Kingston 10
Website: www.jamaicatradeandinvest.org
Telephone # 978-7755

Jamaica Customs
Myers Wharf, Newport East
Kingston 15
Website: www.jacustoms.gov.jm
Telephone #922-5140-8

Trade Board
10th Floor Air Jamaica Building
72 Harbour Street
Kingston
Email: info@tradeboard.gov.jm
Website: www.tradeboard.gov.jm
Telephone #967-0507

National Insurance Scheme
Ministry of Labour & Social Security
18 Ripon Road
Kingston 5
Website: mlss.gov.jm
Telephone # 929-7144-6

HEART Trust/NTA
6B Oxford Road
Kingston 5
Email: info@heart-nta.org
Website: www.heart-nta.org
Telephone # 929-3410-8

National Housing Trust
4 Park Boulevard
Kingston 5
Email: wecare@nht.gov.jm
Website: www.nht.gov.jm
Telephone #929-6500

IMPORTANT AGENCY CONTACTS CONT'D

Jamaica Business Development Corporation
14 Camp Road
Kingston 4
Email: info@jbdc.net
Website: www.jbdc.net
Telephone # 928-5161-5

Jamaica Exporters Association
1 Winchester Road
Kingston 10
Email: info@exportja.org
Website: www.exportja.com
Telephone # 920-6702

WEConnect International in Jamaica
Unit 18 Winchester Business Centre
Kingston
Jamaica
Email: natalee.futureservices@gmail.com
Website: www.weconnectinternational.org
Telephone #906-9553

Heneka Watkis-Porter

Caribbean Export Development Agency
Baobab Tower, Warrens
Barbados
Email: info@carib-export.com
Website: www.carib-export.com
Telephone #1(246) 436-0578